Doc Rivers: The Inspiring Life and Leadership Lessons of One of Basketball's Greatest Coaches

An Unauthorized Biography & Leadership Case Study

By: Clayton Geoffreys

Copyright © 2017 by Calvintir Books, LLC

All rights reserved. Neither this book nor any portion thereof may be reproduced or used in any manner whatsoever without the express written permission. Published in the United States of America.

Disclaimer: The following book is for entertainment and informational purposes only. The information presented is without contract or any type of guarantee assurance. While every caution has been taken to provide accurate and current information, it is solely the reader's responsibility to check all information contained in this article before relying upon it. Neither the author nor publisher can be held accountable for any errors or omissions.

Under no circumstances will any legal responsibility or blame be held against the author or publisher for any reparation, damages, or monetary loss due to the information presented, either directly or indirectly. This book is not intended as legal or medical advice. If any such specialized advice is needed, seek a qualified individual for help.

Trademarks are used without permission. Use of the trademark is not authorized by, associated with, or sponsored by the trademark owners. All trademarks and brands used within this book are used with no intent to infringe on the trademark owners and only used for clarifying purposes.

This book is not sponsored by or affiliated with the National Basketball Association, its teams, the players, coaches, or anyone involved with them.

Visit my website at www.claytongeoffreys.com
Cover photo by Keith Allison is licensed under CC BY 2.0 / modified from original

Table of Contents

Foreword 1

Introduction 3

Chapter 1: Background 10

Chapter 2: Coaching Career 14

    Orlando Magic (1999-2003) 14

    Boston Celtics (2004-2013) 24

    Los Angeles Clippers (2013-Present) 45

Chapter 3: What Makes Doc Rivers a Good Leader 61

    Magic with the Magic 61

    The Ubuntu Philosophy 73

    The Voice of Motivation 80

Chapter 4: How Doc Rivers Maximizes Player Talent 85

    Player Relationship 85

    The Keys to Talent Maximization 90

    The Challenge 98

Chapter 5: Doc Rivers' System 103

Chapter 6: Key Takeaways 110

    Ubuntu 110

    Motivating by Challenging 112

    Treasuring Relationships 114

Conclusion.. 118

Final Word/About the Author 122

References 125

Foreword

When Doc Rivers was named the head coach of the Orlando Magic in 1999, the Magic were in a tough situation. Still reeling from the loss of its two superstars Shaquille O'Neal and Penny Hardaway, the Magic were projected to finish last in the league. Doc Rivers had different plans. He took a team comprised of no stars and translated the season into a near playoff birth. In his first year as a head coach, Doc Rivers would win the Coach of the Year award. Since that first year with the Magic, Doc Rivers has remained one of the most prominent coaches in the NBA due to his ability to lead different star personalities and create a strong sense of team buy-in. His most notable coaching success came in 2008, when he led the Boston Celtics to their first championship since 1986. Thank you for purchasing my book. In this unauthorized biography and leadership case study, we will learn some of the background behind Doc's incredible life story, and more importantly his impact on the game of basketball. In the last section of the book, we'll learn what makes Doc such an effective leader and coach, including a review of key takeaways that you can remember when looking to apply lessons from Doc to your own life. Hope you enjoy and if you do, please do not forget to leave a review!

Also, check out my website at claytongeoffreys.com to join my exclusive list where I let you know about my latest books. To thank you for your purchase, you can go to my site to download a free copy of *33 Life Lessons: Success Principles, Career Advice & Habits of Successful People*. In the book, you'll learn from some of the greatest thought leaders of different industries on what it takes to become successful and how to live a great life.

Cheers,

Clayton Geoffreys

Visit me at www.claytongeoffreys.com

Introduction

NBA coaches are known for being the best basketball strategists in the entire world of professional sports. No coach gets to the NBA if he has not mastered the basic X's and O's of basketball. However, a sound strategy is not the only way a coach succeeds in the NBA. A lot of other factors come into play. An NBA head coach should be able to lead his team through philosophies and other intangibles. Then there is also how the coach manages his rotations and maximizes his players' talents. The financial aspect of managing contracts is also one of the more challenging aspects of coaching in the NBA among others.

If anything, strategy might be the easier part of being a head coach in the NBA because there are several more other factors he has to take into consideration. Most head coaches would sometimes delegate the X's and O's to their assistants so as to focus on the other factors of being the primary voice of leadership of the team. A coach may be the brightest mind as far as strategy is considered but may fail in the other aspects that truly make him great.

One of the harder parts of being a head coach is how to handle the sheer amount of talent he has on his roster. There those that have not been blessed with an All-Star or two on his team. Such coaches rely more on team play and role delegation rather than on how a particular player can take control at any time. There are those that have multiple All-Stars that play well with each other and off one another to the point that chemistry no longer becomes an issue. The difficulty lies in handling one or more transcendent superstars on the team.

Coaches handling several superstars in a loaded team is not a novelty in the NBA. KC Jones was able to have Larry Bird mesh well with Robert Parish and Kevin McHale. Phil Jackson coached both Michael

Jordan and Scottie Pippen to six championships. He then led Kobe Bryant and Shaquille O'Neal to three titles with the Lakers.

In today's NBA, no other head coach in the league has had to try to mesh a lot of talented superstars together in one team than Doc Rivers has had. Since starting out as a head coach in the NBA, Rivers has had to deal with teams that have had multiple superstars and former All-Stars at one or more seasons. In Orlando, he had to make transcendent talent Tracy McGrady mesh well with the likes of the rising Mike Miller and the talented but often injured Grant Hill as well as veteran former All-Stars such as Horace Grant and Shawn Kemp. Rivers did well at that despite being relatively young for a head coach.

Then, when Doc Rivers moved to lead the Boston Celtics, he would toil with coaching only one superstar in Paul Pierce until 2007 when the franchise made moves to acquire superstars Kevin Garnett and Ray

Allen. In less than a year, he was able to make the new Boston Big Three forget about egos and individual accolades for the sake of the all-important NBA championship. The Celtics would go on to win 66 games that season and beat the Lakers in the NBA Finals to grab his first NBA title.

Rivers would continue to lead the Boston Celtics to several more successful seasons. The already talented Big Three would become a foursome of stars when point guard Rajon Rondo rose up to become an All-Star and elite player in his right. In 2010, he would lead such a talented roster that also had a collection of several NBA veterans to the NBA Finals only to lose to the Lakers.

After nine seasons with the Boston Celtics, Doc Rivers would move on to become the head coach of the Los Angeles Clippers. The Clippers that time also had a collection of talented players, who were all young or at the prime of their respective careers. Rivers was going to work his magic on making a core of Chris Paul, Blake Griffin, and DeAndre Jordan into champions, much like how he did with the Boston Big Three.

The way that Doc Rivers has been able to handle talent and superstar egos has been nothing short of spectacular. He allowed Tracy McGrady to thrive and become a superstar in Boston despite the presence of several other veterans that were also stars at some point in their careers. In Boston, he got Pierce, Garnett, and Allen working well together by giving them specific roles and by ingraining into their heads the concept of team play. Kevin Garnett was the defensive and vocal leader of the team. Ray Allen was their go-to perimeter sniper. Paul Pierce was the man to give the ball to in tough situations. Rivers had his stars live the concept of "Ubuntu," which is an African word that relates to respect, unselfishness, community, and sharing.

And when Rajon Rondo rose to become an elite point guard in the NBA, Rivers' Ubuntu lived well within him. Rondo's mentality as a point guard was to make his teammates better and share the ball as much as he could while creating plays for teammates. Under Rivers, Rondo led the NBA in assists twice and would have his best seasons playing for the Celtics.

Even when Doc Rivers moved on to coach the Los Angeles Clippers, his concept of Ubuntu lived on. Both Chris Paul and Blake Griffin are capable enough superstars to be able to put up huge numbers every single night while hogging every play and possession in the process. But both Paul and Griffin took Ubuntu to heart by making winning their priority. The amount of ball sharing and team play they did enabled DeAndre Jordan to rise and become an elite NBA center.

Today, Doc Rivers is only one of six active coaches that have won NBA titles. The others are Gregg

Popovich, Erik Spoelstra, Rick Carlisle, Steve Kerr, and Ty Lue. Rivers has consistently been a winning coach, and he has led teams full of superstars into believing in the team concept and importance of community. He has been considered one of the greatest NBA coaches of his time and is still one of the more sought-after leaders in the league as the game of basketball continues to evolve and change over the years.

Chapter 1: Background

Glenn Anton Rivers was born on October 13, 1961, in Chicago, Illinois to parents Grady and Betty Rivers. Growing up in Maywood, Illinois, he was only known as Glenn Rivers for much of his life, even when he became a high school star at Proviso East High School. At a young age, it was clear that professional sports and basketball ran in Rivers' blood. His uncle was Jim Brewer, who spent nine seasons as a power forward in the NBA and would win a title with the Lakers back in 1982. His cousin, Byron Irvin, would later play in the NBA for three seasons.

Rivers would star in Proviso East High School and would be named a McDonald's All-American. Because of his high school accolades, Rivers would join Marquette University in Milwaukee. It was then and there when Rivers was given the nickname "Doc" by Marquette assistant coach Rick Majerus after he was seen wearing a Julius "Dr. J" Erving shirt in one of their camps. The nickname would stick with him from then on.

Doc Rivers would have a stellar freshman year as a point guard for the Marquette Golden Eagles. He averaged 14 points, a little less than four assists, and 2 steals that season. The following year, he would take his skills to the next level as a star for Marquette. His defense made him a valuable member of the Golden Eagles. He would average 14.3 points, 5.9 assists, and 2.2 steals that season.

After another productive season with Marquette, Doc Rivers would be named a part of the United States basketball team that would go to Colombia for the FIBA World Championship. Rivers averaged nearly 17 points to lead the team in scoring. He would miss what would have been a gold medal winning shot in the waning seconds of the final game. Because of that, Rivers and USA had to settle for the silver medal.

In his junior year with Marquette, Doc Rivers would average 13.2 points, 4.3 assists, and 2.7 steals. In three years with Marquette, he would average 13.9 points, 3.3 rebounds, and 4.6 assists. He would try his hand at the NBA Draft soon after and would get drafted by the Atlanta Hawks with the seventh pick in the second round in 1983.

Doc Rivers would turn out to be a second round steal after proving he was good enough to be the starting point guard for the Atlanta Hawks. He was valued for his defense and ability to find open teammates. In his fourth season in the league, he would average a double-double of 12.8 points and ten assists. Rivers spent much of his time guarding opposing point guards and feeding passes to All-Star Dominique Wilkins. The following year, during the 1987-88 season, Doc Rivers was named to his first and lone All-Star Game averaging 14.2 points, 4.6 rebounds, 9.3 assists, and 1.8 steals.

After spending his first eight seasons with the Atlanta Hawks, wherein he averaged 13 points and 6.8 assists, Doc Rivers would make a single-season stop in Los Angeles as a Clipper. He averaged 10.9 points and 3.9 assists as a 30-year-old point guard that season. He then went to New York, where he spent most of his time on the injured list. Then, in 1994, he was traded to the San Antonio Spurs, where he would spend his final two seasons in the NBA.

Doc Rivers would retire as a player from the game of basketball at the age of 34 after the 1995-96 season as a Spur. For his career, he played 864 games mostly as a starter while averaging 10.9 points, 5.7 rebounds, and 1.8 steals. He retired from the game as the Atlanta Hawks' all-time leader in assists. His record still stands to date. Rivers would have a total of 4,889 career assists and 1,563 steals, which ranks him 34th overall in NBA history.

Chapter 2: Coaching Career

Orlando Magic (1999-2003)

During the 1999 season, which was shortened by a lockout, the Orlando Magic found momentary success after guards Penny Hardaway and Nick Anderson were able to lead the team to tie the best record in the Eastern Conference even without a superstar like Shaq. However, they would lose to the Philadelphia 76ers as early as the first round. After that, it was evident to Magic executives that they needed to start fresh.

The 1999-2000 season was the start of a rebuilding era for the Orlando Magic. They were still recovering from the Shaq era after O'Neal left the team back in 1996. And in the offseason, they had just traded away star guard Penny Hardaway to the Phoenix Suns in exchange for virtually nothing. What remained of the team was essentially a group of role players and guys that were even undrafted. Almost nothing remained of the 1999 team that tied the best record in the East. It was a fresh start for the Magic, and such a fresh start would be marked by the hiring of then 38-year-old Doc Rivers as the new head coach of the team.

Nobody expected much from a team that started four undrafted players and one veteran role player. Fans, team officials, and the entire league had low expectations for the Orlando Magic, who were then speculated to fall near the bottom of the East at the end of the season. For Doc Rivers, there were low expectations on the shoulders of the rookie head coach. He was not slated to save the franchise or continue the success they had seen over the past few seasons. What was expected of him, however, was to grow with the team.

One of the first things that Doc Rivers told the team was that Sports Illustrated expected them to finish the season with the most losses in NBA history. Everyone outside the team expected it to be so. After all, they were a rebuilding team. They wanted one of the top overall picks and to shell off money for free agency. But Doc Rivers did not think of it that way. He approached that season differently. He shunned all external expectations and focused on what the team expected internally. Rivers and the Magic saw losses as unacceptable. The veterans went along with him.[i]

Doc Rivers' best players that season were 31-year-old Darrel Armstrong, an inexperienced Ben Wallace, and veterans Monty Williams and John Amaechi, the latter of which was not even in the NBA the last three seasons. Financially, the entire roster was only worth $17 million, which is what one single superstar was worth back then. On paper, the Orlando Magic did indeed look like they could compete against the best or even the mediocre teams in the league. But they did, and it was all thanks to Doc Rivers.

Showing how good of a motivator he is, Doc Rivers implanted into the minds of his players the mantra, "Heart and Hustle." The young head coach had his team fighting and expecting to win every game they played. It was a group of veterans and young players that nobody else wanted, and yet Rivers made them into fighters and believers. They did not do well on the offensive end, nor were they a great defensive squad. But they had a never-say-die attitude that kept them fighting.[i]

Near the end of the season, the Orlando Magic had a chance to make the playoffs. They would lose an all-important game to the Milwaukee Bucks that would have qualified them for the playoffs. Everyone on the team was crying after that loss. But at the end of it all, a team that was slated to lose more times than any other team in league history has, won half of the 82 games they played that season. Doc Rivers had led a ragtag team of misfits to a 41-41 record on the strength of their heart alone. Because what he was able to accomplish that season, Doc Rivers was named the NBA's Coach of the Year in 2000.

After that season, all the cap space that the Orlando Magic had shelled off the past year paid dividends for the team. They had enough money to sign three max contracts and would aim for big names such as Tim Duncan, Tracy McGrady, and Grant Hill after a season of letting Doc Rivers toil with such a weak roster that only boasted its heart and hustle.

That time, Tim Duncan was the league's fastest-rising big man. He already won a title back in 1999. Grant Hill, on the other hand, was the league's premier small forward. He was the original do-it-all athletic forward that put up triple-doubles in a hurry. Then there was Tracy McGrady, who came out of high school as the most dominant prep player the world has ever seen. In Toronto however, he would spend much of his time playing second fiddle to his cousin Vince Carter.

The Orlando Magic were unable to lure Duncan out of San Antonio, where he would spend the entirety of his career. However, they were able to sign both Grant

Hill and Tracy McGrady to form what would have been the league's most dominant wing duo. Orlando would also acquire a promising Mike Miller off the 2000 NBA Draft. With Hill and T-Mac signed, Doc Rivers was in a position where he had to coach and handle two big-name stars. But what was important was that he no longer had to make do with a mediocre roster because he already had two stars to work with and one other promising wing that could pay dividends for him.

Unfortunately for Doc Rivers, a severe ankle injury limited Grant Hill to only four games the entire season. Hill would have been the do-it-all star he could have leaned on during his second season of coaching the Orlando Magic. Instead, it was Tracy McGrady who rose to the occasion and would become one of the premier scoring wingmen in the entire league. From averaging 15.4 points as Vince Carter's backup in Toronto, McGrady blossomed into a star that averaged nearly 27 points for the Magic. T-Mac would win the

Most Improved Player award. Meanwhile, rookie Mike Miller turned out to be the best-performing newcomer that season and would win the NBA's Rookie of the Year award.

Having go-to guys with him, Doc Rivers' heart and hustle era lasted for merely a year as the team would rely on its stars for much of the heavy lifting. The Orlando Magic would see a return to the playoffs with a record of 43 wins as against 39 losses. They would qualify as the seventh seed in the East. However, Orlando would see its postseason appearance cut short when the Milwaukee Bucks defeated them in the first round in only four games.

There was not much of a roster change the following season for Doc Rivers' Orlando Magic. While T-Mac continued to improve as a superstar, Grant Hill was still yet to pay dividends for the hefty sum he was signed up for by the Magic. Hill was again limited that season playing only 14 total games. The team still relied on T-Mac and Miller to take them further than they ever did.

Doc Rivers had his team playing a high-octane type of offense that relied a lot on the three-point shot. Orlando was third in the entire league in three-pointers made while ranking second overall in most attempts from the outside. The Magic would end up ranking fourth overall in offense by the end of the season and would win one more game than they did the previous year. The 44-38 Orlando Magic would make the playoffs as the fifth seed in the East. However, Rivers and his squad would get booted out of the first round in only four games by the Charlotte Hornets.

During the 2002-03 season, Grant Hill never played a single game and did not even suit up for the team because of what appeared to be a career-ending ankle injury. But Tracy McGrady would rise to become the league's best scorer. Rivers relied on T-Mac to do everything. The Magic superstar scored, rebounded, and assisted at high levels. And with Mike Miller traded midseason, McGrady's scoring only increased even more.

Doc Rivers allowed T-Mac to flourish into arguably the league's best individual player that season. He averaged more than 32 points, 6.5 rebounds, and 5.5 assists for the Magic. Rivers and McGrady would, however, struggle to make the playoffs. They would win only 42 games and would qualify as the eighth seed in the East.

The eighth-seeded Orlando Magic that Doc Rivers led to the playoffs seemed gritty and intent on pulling off an upset against a powerful defensive unit such as the Detroit Pistons. Banking on T-Mac's superstar high, Doc Rivers opened up the series 1-0 by stealing Game 1 away from the Pistons. After losing Game 2, Rivers coached the Magic to defend their home court and would lead the series 3-1 after Game 4.

After that win in Game 4, it seemed as if Tracy McGrady jinxed the team. T-Mac, who had never reached the second round of the playoffs at that point in his career, told reporters that it felt great that he was finally going to the second round even though the series was still far from over. After that, the Pistons would go on to win three consecutive games to end the series in seven games.

The 2003-04 season would turn out to be the final one for Doc Rivers as the head coach of the Orlando Magic. During the offseason, the team acquired capable veterans Juwan Howard and Ty Lue to back T-Mac up. However, things did not turn out the way they wanted them to. After winning his first game during that season, Doc Rivers would end up losing ten consecutive outings. With a 1-10 start under his belt that season, Doc Rivers was fired. The Magic would extend their losing streak to 19 games and would end the season with the NBA's worst record.

After five seasons with the Orlando Magic, Doc Rivers had a subpar and mediocre win-loss record of 171-168. It was not the most impressive record by any measure. However, Doc Rivers was able to make do with what was given to him. He was the 2000 NBA Coach of the Year after the impressive coaching job he did with what was considered one of the less talented rosters on paper. He then coached Tracy McGrady to superstardom while also managing an injury-laden roster that solely relied on their best player for the heavy lifting.

Boston Celtics (2004-2013)

After getting fired by the Orlando Magic, Doc Rivers would spend an entire season as a television broadcaster. He was even a part of the broadcast team that called the 2004 NBA Finals. However, he would not spend time working for television for too long considering that his commitment with the Magic and the way he has coached that team, especially during the 1999-2000 season, got him the attention of another franchise seeking to move on to a new kind of leadership.

After the 2004 playoffs, the Boston Celtics dismissed then interim coach John Carroll. General manager Danny Ainge would announce that he was not in a hurry to hire a new coach, but would immediately find a suitable replacement in the form of Doc Rivers, who he said was the man the team sorely wanted to be the Celtics' new head coach.[ii]

For Doc Rivers, he found that it was an easy decision to accept the job after Danny Ainge called him and offered the job to him. Because the Boston Celtics are arguably the most storied franchise in the history of the NBA, Rivers did not have a reason to say no to the job.[ii] After all, he did play in the NBA during the era of Larry Bird. He saw firsthand how the Celtics won championships in the 80's and how they booted him and his Hawks out of the playoffs in a historic series back in 1988.

Doc Rivers came into a good situation when he started to coach the Boston Celtics. Star Paul Pierce was in the prime of his career. He was backed up by scoring specialist Ricky Davis and an old but still active Gary Payton. They also had youngsters Al Jefferson and Tony Allen, who would both become productive players in their right. The team already had good pieces. Doc Rivers was thought to be the missing part of that puzzle.

During the 2004-05 season, Doc Rivers led the Boston Celtics to become one of the highest-scoring teams in the league. Highlighted by All-Star Paul Pierce, Boston finished the season as the fifth highest scoring team in the entire league. Rivers would lead the team to a 45-37 finish, which was his highest thus far as a coach. They would also finish with the third seed in the East. For the first time as a head coach, Doc Rivers would have homecourt advantage in the first round.

However, Doc Rivers would fail to make use of his homecourt advantage. After winning Game 1 in Boston, the Celtics would end up losing Game 2 at home. They would take Game 4 away from the Indiana Pacers, their first round opponents, but would also lose their advantage again in Game 5. After forcing Game 7 with a win in Indianapolis, the Celtics would lose the series on their home floor when the Pacers blew them out. The Celtics were merely 1-3 in the four home games they played in that series.

The 2005-06 season was a rather tough one for Doc Rivers. The Celtics would continue to trade away some of their productive pieces in exchange for new players. Veteran Antoine Walker was traded during the offseason while Ricky Davis was sent to Minnesota in exchange for Wally Szczerbiak. The team also underwent various roster reshuffling due to trades and other strategic changes that Doc Rivers saw fit. The only players that remained constants were star player Paul Pierce and rising guard Delonte West.

Paul Pierce would have his best individual season as a superstar averaging nearly 27 points the entire season. However, Pierce's career season was for naught after the Celtics would fail to make the playoffs. After a successful first season in Boston, Doc Rivers would end up only winning 33 out of their 82 games during the 2005-06 season. For the third time in his career as a head coach, Doc Rivers would miss the playoffs.

The Boston Celtics' luck continued to run out during the 2006-07 season though they were able to build well through the draft when they took point guard Rajon Rondo with their first-round pick. The unfortunate part was that Paul Pierce had suffered a foot injury, which put the Celtics in a 2-22 record over the 24 games that he missed. Moreover, productive guard Tony Allen would tear his ACL after a dunk. Because of that,

Rivers would turn to rising center Al Jefferson as his go-to guy for much of that season. The result was a 24-58 record for Doc Rivers and the unlucky Boston Celtics.

The two unlucky and unsuccessful seasons for the Boston Celtics would pay dividends in the offseason of 2007. Danny Ainge would make a series of moves that would revitalize the franchise and give Doc Rivers two more stars in his lineup. In the modern day era of the Boston Celtics, those moves were arguably what brought the team back to prominence for the first time since the 80's.

First, Ainge would draft capable forward Jeff Green with the fifth overall pick of the 2007 NBA Draft. With Jeff Green as the centerpiece of the trade, the Celtics would send the rookie, Szczerbiak, and West over to Seattle in exchange for multiple-time All-Star and arguably the best shooter of his generation Ray Allen. Then, Ainge would commune with his former

Celtic teammate Kevin McHale, who was the general manager of the Minnesota Timberwolves back then.

McHale discussed with Ainge a trade that involved 2004 MVP, Kevin Garnett. While Garnett was happy with Minnesota, the team ownership felt that they needed to let their franchise player go to chase titles that he could win if he had chosen to stay with the Timberwolves. Because of that, the Celtics would send Gerald Green, Ryan Gomes, Al Jefferson, and several other role players in exchange for the services of the Big Ticket.

With Ray Allen and Kevin Garnett teaming up together with Paul Pierce in Boston, the Celtics would have a new modern day version of the Big Three. This was the move that made the Boston Celtics relevant again. And for Doc Rivers, this team led by the Big Three was what made him known as one of the most elite coaches in the NBA at that time.

Despite having three superstars over in Boston, there were several challenges that Doc Rivers had to overcome during the offseason and regular season itself. The first one, of course, was managing the egos of his three stars. Pierce, Allen, and Garnett were all used to be the leading men when they were lone superstars. Though they managed well playing with other players that were also All-Stars at one point in their careers, playing with two other superstars was an entirely different story. This was how Doc Rivers' "Ubuntu" started.

The Boston Celtics would have a trip to Rome during the offseason as part of the NBA's European tour. It was that time when the Big Three bonded together and experienced what Ubuntu was. Ubuntu, an African word, has no exact meaning in the English language. However, the concept has a universal thought to it. It stresses community, sharing, and how collective success is much more important that individual achievements.[iii]

Pretty soon, Doc Rivers adopted Ubuntu as the team's battle cry before games. He had previously learned about the concept by reading works by Bishop Desmond Tutu.[iii] He loved the meaning of it and wanted his players to live by it. The good thing was that it did not take long for the entire Celtics and not just the Big Three to embrace Ubuntu as their motto and battle cry.

As the season unfolded, it immediately became apparent that the Boston Celtics' Big Three worked well, not just with one another, but also with their role players Rajon Rondo, Kendrick Perkins, and a bench full of veterans aching for a title. What was also obvious was how Doc Rivers suddenly changed his style to fit the profile of the Celtics' roster.

When he was in Orlando and during his earlier years as the Celtics' head coach, Doc Rivers stressed the offensive part of the game more than he did the defensive end. Tracy McGrady and the other Magic players were consistently leading the team to high-scoring outputs. Meanwhile, Paul Pierce at his prime together with other high-scoring players paved the way for the Celtics to become one of the top offensive teams in the league during Rivers' first year in Boston. Doc Rivers almost always relied on the prowess of his superstars back then.

However, during the 2007-08 season, Doc Rivers turned the Boston Celtics into an elite defensive unit that stressed the importance of suffocating defense to win games. Rivers himself was a great defender back when he was still playing. He would bring the same kind of defensive intensity with him to the Celtics that season.

But the beauty about Boston's defense that season was that it was just as team-oriented as their offense. Aside from Kevin Garnett and James Posey, no other player in the lineup was renowned for their defensive abilities. The younger versions of Kendrick Perkins, Rajon

Rondo, and Tony Allen were still growing and learning as defenders back then. What made them an elite defensive team was that they helped each other out and communicated well to the tune of Ubuntu, or unity.

Doc Rivers was described as the ultimate players' coach. He communicated well with his players and made them feel like family and friends. That was how he made his Big Three play specific roles that fit their strengths. Ray Allen would spend much of his time waiting outside the perimeter for shot opportunities. Paul Pierce was the offensive creator that broke defenses down. Meanwhile, Kevin Garnett was the man that anchored the defensive end well enough that he would win the Defensive Player of the Year award at the end of the season.

Nobody expected the Big Three to gel well together in less than a year. Doc Rivers made sure that they forgot their goals for the sake of winning a title. But another difficult part of coaching that team was that Rivers also had to handle the growth and development of his younger players Rondo, Tony Allen, and Perkins. Though the focus was pointed more towards the Big Three, Rivers was still able to help his younger players grow into capable players themselves.

At the end of the season, the Boston Celtics ranked on top of the league in nearly every defensive statistic. They suffocated teams to low scoring outputs while also scoring the ball well themselves. That was what allowed the Celtics to win 66 games and complete what was then the greatest single-season turnaround made by any franchise. The Boston Celtics improved by 42 wins from a season prior. While it was expected of them to be contenders, the work that Doc Rivers did with that roster turned the Celtics into dominant title favorites.

The road to the championship was not easy, however. Boston had to endure a seven-game series against the eighth-seeded Atlanta Hawks in the first round. With that win, Rivers was able to get to the second round of the playoffs for the first time in his career as a head coach. He would move even further by battling the Cleveland Cavaliers to another seven-game series. They would then beat the Detroit Pistons in six games to reach the NBA Finals for the first time 1987 when Larry Bird was still leading the original Big Three.

The last time the Celtics made the NBA Finals, they were against the Lakers. More than two decades later, the two teams would square off again for NBA supremacy as the two most storied franchises would battle for the championship. On one end, Doc Rivers led the charge together with his Big Three. On the opposing side, the legendary nine-time NBA champion Phil Jackson was gunning for his tenth title while leading Kobe Bryant, who was aiming for his fourth ring.

After six games, the dust settled, and Doc Rivers won his first NBA title together with the Big Three, who were all champions for the first time in their careers. The title win marked the 17th NBA championship for the Boston Celtics, who still leads the league in that category. It was also their first NBA title since 1986, which was 22 years ago from 2008.

Being on top of the NBA food chain meant that Doc Rivers and the Boston Celtics had large targets on their back. Despite the aging roster and the rise of other superstars in other Eastern teams such as Dwight Howard of the Orlando Magic and LeBron James of the Cleveland Cavaliers, the Celtics maintained their hold on the top record in the NBA before they would see a momentary breakdown due to Kevin Garnett's injury. The loss of Garnett was painful for the Celtics, who would end the regular season as the second seed in the East. Garnett's injury would have an even bigger effect on them during the postseason.

Without their anchor on the defensive end, the Boston Celtics struggled against the seventh-seeded Chicago Bulls in the first round. They would win in seven games and with many overtime periods. Then, in the second round, Garnett's ability to defend the paint would have been useful in limiting Dwight Howard, who dominated the series. The Orlando Magic would end up beating the Boston Celtics in seven games and would meet and lose to the Lakers later on in the NBA Finals.

The Boston Celtics would start with a 23-5 record during the 2009-10 season. However, Doc Rivers would then be criticized for a move he deemed to be in the interests of the team's long-term health. Knowing he had an aging core of Pierce, Allen, and Garnett, Rivers would lessen his starters' minutes and give more time to his bench and role players. This move allowed Rajon Rondo to blossom into an All-Star as he would own the spotlight when the Big Three were resting.

After that hot start, the Boston Celtics cooled down and would end up with a 27-27 record in their final 54 games of the regular season. They would finish the campaign with 50 wins as against 32 losses. Nobody expected the Boston Celtics to do well in the playoffs considering how pedestrian they were during the latter part of the regular season. However, they would manage to do well.

With his starters well-rested thanks to the decreased playing time he gave his core players during the regular season, Doc Rivers looked like a genius in the playoffs. The Celtics dominated the Miami Heat in five games to score a meeting with the MVP LeBron James and the top-seeded Cleveland Cavaliers in the second round. With a healthy lineup and their suffocating defense, the Celtics made James look human as he looked like he quit on his team. Doc Rivers would coach his team to a 4-2 win in that series. And in the Conference Finals, they exacted revenge against the Orlando Magic, who they beat in six games to reach the NBA Finals for the second time in three years.

The 2010 NBA Finals was again a battle between the two storied rivals. The Lakers were the defending champions and were the favorites against an older but wiser Celtics team. It was also a duel between a man who has won a historically best 10 NBA titles as a coach and Doc Rivers, who was still on the high of winning his first and only title in 2008.

That series turned out to be tighter than the lopsided contest they had in 2008. They were trading wins with each other. At one point, the Celtics were up 3-2 in the series heading into Game 6. But it was in that blowout loss in Game 6 when the Celtics lost Kendrick Perkins to a severe injury. While Perkins was not statistically Doc Rivers' best asset in the center position, he brought a lot of defensive intangibles to the team. In Game 7, his ability to box opposing big men out and set good screens was sorely missed as the Lakers won a defensive battle to win the 2010 NBA title.

While Doc Rivers' Boston Celtics remained powerhouse contenders in the East throughout the 2010-11 season, it was clear that they had met their match in the conference. Three of the top superstars in the NBA banded together to form a younger and better trio than the one the Celtics had. LeBron James, Dwyane Wade, and Chris Bosh were a younger and more talented trio than nearly any other formed in the history of the league.

With the emergence of Rajon Rondo as an All-Star, the Boston Celtics won 56 games during the regular season and were primed for another shot at the NBA title. Knowing how much his team had slowed down, Doc Rivers preached defense night in and night out to try and make for his aging core. The league's top defensive team would dominate the New York Knicks in the first round of the 2011 playoffs.

However, in the second round, they would meet the Miami Heat. The Miami Heat had been ousted by the Celtics in the playoffs the last season. But they only had Dwyane Wade that time. This time, Wade recruited Bosh and James, who the Celtics also defeated a year prior in the playoffs. Doc Rivers' demons chased him and formed an equally if not more devastating trio to counter the one he had with him in Boston. The Miami Heat would pounce on the slower and older Celtics and would beat them in only five games.

The 2011-12 season would be the last hurrah for Doc Rivers' Big Three in Boston. The long offseason due to the lockout had given his aging group of veterans ample time to rest and recover the bones and muscles that had been banged up from all the physical battles they had fought since 2007. The Big Three and Rondo would win 39 out of the 66 regular season games they played that season. But what had become evident was that the team was old and way past its prime. Nobody expected them to go far in the playoffs.

Doc Rivers would have a tough time dispatching the Atlanta Hawks in the first round. The Boston Celtics had to fight six games with them to reach the second round, where they saw a fierce battle against the Philadelphia 76ers. The Sixers forced them to seven games but would still end up on the short end of the stick after the Celtics used their experience to their advantage.

In the Eastern Conference Finals, everybody expected the Miami Heat to run over the Boston Celtics the same way they did a year before. However, nobody expected the fight that Rivers had ingrained into the minds of his players. With Ubuntu as their battle cry, the Celtics trio suffocated the Heat defensively and would force them into relying more on LeBron James. They would manage to force seven games out of the Miami Heat and led the series 3-2 at one point. Despite the tough fight they gave, the Heat were younger and more talented than they were at that point. Rivers' Ubuntu was what kept the team going, but it was not enough.

During the offseason of 2012, the Celtics' belief on the Ubuntu that Doc Rivers kept on preaching was falling. Reports went on that Rajon Rondo did not gel well with any other person on the roster. He had no friends in the team and was rumored to have been internally feuding with Ray Allen. And at the very worse, he almost even had a fight with Doc Rivers at one point.[iii]

Fed up with Rajon Rondo's increasing ego and the Boston Celtics' inability to win another title, Ray Allen left during the offseason to join none other than the rival Miami Heat team. Ray Allen's departure marked the slow falling out of Doc Rivers, his core of veterans, and the Big Three era of the Boston Celtics. Rumors were circulating that the Celtics front office were thinking of heading in a new direction. Reports came out that they were having talks with other teams to trade both Pierce and Garnett. Of course, Rivers would naturally also want out of Boston if such a scenario happened.

Nevertheless, no trade and no resignation happened during the 2012-13 season. Rivers would lead the Celtics to a subpar 41-40 record during the regular season. The team's defense had fallen off. They were no longer playing with the sense of Ubuntu that Rivers had long been preaching to them since 2007. The Boston Celtics would eventually lose to the New York Knicks in six games in the first round of the 2013 playoffs.

During the offseason of 2013, Doc Rivers was allowed by the Boston Celtics out of his contract so that he could go to Los Angeles to coach the Clippers. In exchange for that, the Clippers gave the Celtics a first-round draft pick in what was essentially a trade for a coach. Not too long after, the Celtics jumpstarted their rebuilding process by trading away both Pierce and Garnett to the Brooklyn Nets. In the nine seasons he spent with Boston, Doc Rivers had a record of 416-305, which gives him a 57.7% winning record. The best run he had with the Celtics, of course, was when he led them to 2008 NBA Championship. Both Rivers and the Celtics have not won more titles ever since.

Los Angeles Clippers (2013-Present)

Doc Rivers would inherit from former head coach Vinny Del Negro a loaded LA Clippers team that was primed to compete for a title with the talent that they had. At point guard, they had Chris Paul, who was considered the best pure playmaker in the game since he broke out in 2007. At power forward, they had the robust and athletic 2011 Rookie of the Year Blake Griffin, who dunks over opponents and dominates his matchup with his mobility every single night. But the X-factor of that team was high-rising center DeAndre

Jordan, whose athletic abilities have never been matched at the center position.

Despite the loaded talent that the Clippers had, they were considered underachievers. Del Negro never fully utilized all that talent and athleticism. Chris Paul was always a creator that was more effective when he had the ball in his hands. Blake Griffin, despite his jaw-dropping athletic abilities, had more skill than what he was given credit for. And if given the minutes and if used correctly, DeAndre Jordan could become a force on both ends of the floor.

In only his rookie season with the LA Clippers, Doc Rivers immediately harnessed all the talent on his roster to make the Clippers one of the best teams not only in the West, but the entire NBA. He also made the Clippers one of the most exciting team to watch as he fully realized the team's moniker as Lob City. With Chris Paul's ability to make plays and with all the athleticism that the frontcourt had, the Clippers played faster and more fluidly under Doc Rivers.

Considered the ultimate motivator and as a player's coach, Doc Rivers imbued more confidence in his core players that no other Clipper coach had ever done before. Chris Paul was back to averaging the 20 points and the ten assists he was averaging back when he was in New Orleans. Blake Griffin had the best scoring season he has ever had in his career. After averaging only 18 points the year before, he upped his scoring to a career best of more than 24 points under Rivers. Backup shooting guard Jamal Crawford also returned to the conversation as the best sixth man in the league. But the biggest effect that Rivers had on the team was how he made DeAndre Jordan improve so much.

DeAndre Jordan came into the league with so much athleticism at the center position that his ability to rise was unmatched by any other player at his position. However, Jordan was never very skillful. He had no go-to moves inside the paint and was dreadfully ungraceful at the post. While he started most of the games for Vinny Del Negro, he did not play enough minutes and was only utilized as a shot blocker and rebounder. In his final year under Del Negro, he only averaged 8.8 points and 7.4 rebounds.

But in only his first season as a Clipper, Doc Rivers was looking for a third head that he could add to the duo of Paul and Griffin. The league was dominated by trios of stars. Rivers wanted his own Big Three in Los Angeles, and he found one in DeAndre Jordan. Doc Rivers would instill a lot of confidence in the athletic center and would challenge him to become one of the top defensive players in the league.

DeAndre Jordan would rise to Doc Rivers' challenge and would become a double-double defensive monster for the LA Clippers. After subpar numbers the last season, Rivers gave him starter's minutes, and he would average 10.4 points, a league-leading 13.6

rebounds, and 2.5 blocks in addition to also leading the league in field goal percentage. Knowing how limited Jordan's offense was, Rivers used him primarily as an inside offense for lob passes from his playmakers and when perimeter players break down the defense and get all the way to the paint.

With both Jordan and Griffin catching lobs from Paul and dunking the ball down with force on a nightly basis, Rivers fully realized the potential of the Clippers of being the league's Lob City. He would lead Los Angeles to a franchise record of 57 wins in the season. He also led the Clippers to become the highest scoring and best offensive team in the league.

Coming into the playoffs as the third seed, the Los Angeles Clippers would face a tough matchup in the sixth-seeded Golden State Warriors, a team that relied a lot on its outside shooting. Fighting against an equally explosive offensive team, the Clippers had it tough in the opening round and would need seven games to beat the Warriors and to advance to the second round.

However, that series was highlighted mainly by the racist comments made by then-Clippers owner Donald Sterling. To this end, Doc Rivers stated publicly that he would not return to the team if Sterling continued as the owner. NBA Commissioner Adam Silver would compel Donald Sterling to sell the franchise after the end of the season.

In the second round, Doc Rivers would realize how much different and more challenging the Western Conference is compared to the East. Coming in as the third seed, they would face a second-seeded Oklahoma City Thunder led by two of the best players the NBA had to offer in Kevin Durant and Russell Westbrook. While Rivers managed to coach the Clippers to steal Game 1 away from OKC, they would cede Games 2 and 3. Despite tying the series up in Game 4, the

Clippers would lose Games 5 and 6 as the Thunder managed their way into the Western Conference Finals.

During the offseason of 2014, Doc Rivers was promoted to become the president of basketball operations of the Los Angeles Clippers while continuing as the team's head coach. This meant that Rivers had the final say in all matters relating to basketball. He would also further extend his contract with the Clippers ensuring that what he had with the team was a long-term commitment.

Doc Rivers continued to coach the LA Clippers as one of the top scoring and exciting teams in the league. While their offense was eventually dwarfed by the much-improved Golden State Warriors, the Clippers were still second in the league in most points scored per game while leading the NBA in offensive rating for the second consecutive season. Doc Rivers did this by letting the concept of Ubuntu live on with his Clippers.

The Los Angeles Clippers continued that selfless philosophy that Doc Rivers endlessly preached to the Boston Celtics since 2008. While the Clippers had designated scorers and playmakers, everyone passed the ball well while also caring less about who scored the most points or who had the best performance. This also led to how Rivers designated his three best players with roles that best fit their skills.

Chris Paul was the alpha and omega of the team; everything started and ended with him. He initiated plays that usually end with him slicing and dishing out to an open teammate or scoring the ball himself. Blake Griffin, who was known to be an explosive double-double machine, became a better all-around player. Rivers used his unique skillset to make him the team's secondary playmaker while retaining his status as the go-to guy for points. Meanwhile, DeAndre Jordan was the man that lorded the paint by collecting rebounds, finishing lob plays and inside passes, and swatting away shots.

By the end of the regular season, one in which Doc Rivers made a move to acquire his son Austin to play for him thus becoming the first coach to coach his son, the Los Angeles Clippers won 56 out of the 82 games they played. They would maintain their hold as one of the top teams in the West as they secured the third seed heading into the postseason.

The first round matchup was not easy, however. Rivers had to face the five-time NBA champion Gregg Popovich and the defending titleholders the San Antonio Spurs early on in the playoffs. The tough challenge of facing the defending champions got to them early on, and the Clippers would start the series on a 1-2 deficit despite having homecourt advantage. Heading into Game 6 on a losing end of the series, the Clippers would manage to force Game 7 where they would win by only two points and make it to the second round for another year under Rivers' leadership.

Doc Rivers would face a former 80's rival in the second round when he went up against the Kevin McHale coached Houston Rockets. That matchup was slated to be one of the better series in the playoffs considering that both teams won 56 games during the regular season and were equal in almost every sense. It was only through a tiebreaker that Houston got the second seed over the Clippers.

Despite playing without homecourt advantage on their side, Rivers and the Clippers stole Game 1 away from Los Angeles and seemed like the better team at that point. They would drop Game 2 but would defend homecourt in Games 3 and 4 to go up 3-1 in the series. Though they already seemed to have the series wrapped up in Game 6 when they were entering the fourth quarter with a huge lead, the Los Angeles Clippers suddenly melted down. The Rockets' bench players suddenly outplayed the entire Clipper roster as Houston completed a monumental run that forced Game 7. In Game 7, the Rockets continued the comeback of the year after winning three straight games to defeat the Los Angeles Clippers, who almost secured the franchise's first-ever appearance in the Conference Finals had they managed to hold on to their lead in Game 6.

The 2015-16 season would be a tough one for Doc Rivers and his LA Clippers. For much of the season, they were without leading scorer Blake Griffin, who suffered an injury late in December 2015. Nevertheless, the LA Clippers held on, even without their leading scorer as the team stayed true to its belief in unity and community rather than individuality. No other player on the team held on to this belief more than Paul Pierce, who was acquired in the offseason as a free agent. At 38 years old, Pierce no longer had what it took to carry a team on his shoulders. But he would, however, find solace in being a veteran presence and a big shot-maker whenever he was needed.

Without Blake Griffin, the Clippers' offense saw a decline. Not only was Griffin an explosive scorer, he was also a superb playmaker. The Clippers would fall from being the second best scoring team in the league to seventh that season. And after two seasons of leading the league in offensive rating, they would fall to eighth. At the end of the regular season, the LA Clippers won 53 games to qualify for the playoffs as the fourth seed in the Western Conference.

In the first round matchup against the Portland Trailblazers, Doc Rivers was lucky enough to have all of his starters in good health, though Griffin was still to return to the peak form that made him one of the best big men in the entire league. In Games 1 and 2, the Blazers seemed completely outmatched and outclassed. There was seemingly no way for them to contend with the firepower of the Clippers.

Luck was quick to rear its ugly head for Doc Rivers. In Game 4, the 2-1 Clippers seemed to be in great shape to go up 3-1 until an injury struck Chris Paul. What was worse was that later on in the game, Blake Griffin would go down with an injury as well. Without their two best players, the Clippers would falter in Game 4 and the rest of the series to fall in the first round for the first time since Doc Rivers took over as the head coach.

The 2016-17 season was a testament to how Doc Rivers handles his personnel and can motivate his players to play more like stars rather than bench guys. Throughout the first 16 games of the season, the Clippers led the league with only two losses under their belts. Not only were they winning, but they also blew their opponents out in nine of those 14 wins.

While the Clippers kept their pace as one of the best teams in the league, Blake Griffin would yet again go down with another injury. In the 18 consecutive games that Griffin missed, the Clippers went 10-8. Despite keeping afloat without their best scorer, the Clippers would again lose another key player when Chris Paul got injured at about the same time as Griffin returned from injury. In the 14 games that Paul missed, LA would only win six games.

What was remarkable about Doc Rivers that season was that despite losing his two best players in two different stretches of the season, he kept the LA Clippers fighting. While Paul and Griffin were their two best stars, Ubuntu meant that the team was more the sum of their two All-Stars and that it was more of a collective effort that made them Western Conference contenders. Doc Rivers saw his son Austin stepping up to the challenge of filling in for Paul while getting the most out of role players such as Luc Mbah a Moute and Marreese Speights, among others.

Despite another injury-plagued season for Doc Rivers and the LA Clippers, the team still locked in homecourt advantage in the first round by earning the fourth seed in the West. The Clippers won 51 games though they missed their two best players for long stretches of the season. It was also that season when DeAndre Jordan rose to become an All-Star.

The Los Angeles Clippers, however, could not contain the Utah Jazz in the first round. Arguably their most equal matchup in the entire Western Conference, the Clippers traded blows with the Jazz until the series reached a seventh and deciding game. In Game 7, however, the Clippers melted down again and would be sent home packing in the first round for a second straight season.

Despite not seeing the same success and dominance with the Clippers compared to when he was in Boston, Doc Rivers was able to make the team compete at a time when the Western Conference was arguably at its toughest thanks to consistently dominant teams such as the Warriors and Spurs. The tougher playing field was not the only reason as to why Rivers found it difficult to break it out of the West.

For most of his third and fourth seasons with the Clippers, Doc Rivers had to keep the ship floating despite injuries to his key players. Moreover, the Los Angeles Clippers found it difficult to plug the hole at the small forward spot, which was thought to be their biggest weakness. But as seen from how they started the 2016-17 season, the Clippers were surely a force under Rivers if only they could stay healthy for the majority of the campaign.

Injuries were what always plagued Doc Rivers' coaching career. He could have had a super lineup in Orlando had Grant Hill been healthy and able to play a full season without getting hurt. A tandem of Hill and McGrady would have been legendary. With the Celtics, a fully healthy lineup in 2008 got Doc Rivers his first and only NBA title. But when injury kept Kevin Garnett out of the playoffs in 2009, Rivers was ousted in the second round. The injury to Kendrick Perkins in the 2010 NBA Finals was what ultimately did the Boston Celtics in. In any case, Doc Rivers' starting five of Rondo, Allen, Pierce, Garnett, and Perkins was never defeated in a playoff series when they were all healthy.

And with the Clippers, aside from the meltdowns that the team suffered, they could have done better had the roster been healthy throughout the last two seasons. But make no mistake. The Clippers are merely healthy season and a capable small forward away from being title contenders under Doc Rivers' leadership.

Chapter 3: What Makes Doc Rivers a Good Leader

Magic with the Magic

Doc Rivers has been around in the NBA since 1999 when he started as a rookie head coach for the Orlando Magic just a few seasons after retiring from the game of basketball as a player. It was not until 2008 when he became known as an elite head coach because of how he led a talent-laden Boston Celtics squad to throw away their egos and believe in the goal of winning a title for the team. Needless to say, 2008 was arguably his most accomplished year as a head coach.

While the 2007-08 season was the campaign that brought Doc Rivers his first and only NBA championship ring, it can also be said that it was not his best year as a leader and coach. Arguably, his best season as a head coach was the time when he had no talent and All-Stars in his team. It was that season when he practically had nothing to work with and had to play with the cards that were dealt to him. It was that fateful 1999-2000 season when he first started out coaching.

In 2000, the Coach of the Year award was not given to the coach with the most wins. It was not even given to the one that led his team to the highest winning improvements. The award was given to the coach that had to make do with the roster of players he had. It was not given to the head coach that made more with more. It was given to Doc Rivers, who made more with less.

During the 1999-2000 season, Doc Rivers was hired to jumpstart the Orlando Magic's rebuilding project. The team had practically nothing. They traded almost the entire roster during the 1999 offseason to shell out a lot of cap space for what was a star-laden 2000 free agency period and to be able to tank and get one of the top draft picks in the following season's NBA Draft. Because of that, Doc Rivers not only had zero All-Stars to deal with but he had to work with a team that had four undrafted players as his starters and a collection of role players that no other team wanted.

With the roster of players that Doc Rivers had coming into the 1999-2000 season, it was expected that the Magic would lose more games than any other team in NBA history. After all, he had one of the worst rosters ever assembled in the annals of the league. And as for him, he was an unproven head coach that had zero experience in coaching, even as an assistant. All he had with him was his background and expertise as a former NBA All-Star guard. Nevertheless, Doc Rivers won half of the games he coached that season and would eventually win the Coach of the Year award for turning trash into gold that season. But exactly how did he do it? Dr. Greg Morris of Leadership Dynamics™ examined and analyzed how he brought that team together to win 41 out of 82 games[iv]:

1. **Set the Bar High**

    The first lesson that Morris believed that Doc Rivers taught to his team during that 1999-2000 season was setting the bar high. He knew what the external expectations were. Other teams expected them to lose big. The media thought they would end up with the most losses in league history. However, Rivers thought that those were merely external. What was important was their internal expectations. He would never let his team believe that they were not good enough. Instead, Doc Rivers wanted his team to expect that they could win every game they played.

Before the season tipped off, Doc Rivers sent all of his players a package that read "Are you committed?" After that, he would send another one that said: "we are going to be the best defensive team in the NBA." For Rivers, it was all about the players' commitment to becoming great. External expectations did not matter to him as long as all of his guys committed to the same goal of believing they could win. He would set the bar high by making them believe that they could beat any other team in the league by becoming the best defensive squad in the NBA.

As history would dictate to us, the Orlando Magic did not become the best defensive team in the league that season. As far as keeping their opponents from scoring was concerned, they were in the middle of the pack. However, they were in the top 10 when it came to defensive rating, which meant that they were a pretty good defensive team. However, they were not the best.

Despite not being the best defensive team that season, the Orlando Magic already overachieved. By setting a goal as high as becoming the best defensive team in the entire NBA, the Orlando Magic continued to aim for a goal that was seemingly impossible to achieve but had the consolation prize of making them an excellent defensive team despite the bad roster of players that they had. The Magic would not reach their goal but would overachieve by setting a standard so high that they thought they could achieve it.

Morris would quote American football great Vince Lombardi on this one. Lombardi once said that "the quality of a person's life is in direct proportion to their commitment to excellence, regardless of their chosen field of endeavor." This meant that when a person tries to achieve excellence in every endeavor they seek, their life would always be more meaningful and fruitful.

For Doc Rivers, he was never satisfied with believing that his team would not achieve and amount to anything during that 1999-2000 season. Nobody can ever be successful by aiming to become mediocre. Instead, good leaders would always strive to help his players or people to aim for excellence. That was what Rivers forced his team to believe in. He made the 1999-2000 Orlando Magic strive for excellence. Despite not making the playoffs that season, winning half of the games they played was already a good enough achievement for a team that nobody expected to amount to anything.

2. Go With What You Got

As the saying goes, "you play with the hand you're dealt." While that saying relates to a game of cards or chance, it relates to life as well. Life deals you with unfortunate circumstances that are well out of your control in certain situations of your life. But it does not mean that you should just succumb to those kinds of situations. Instead, you play with whatever hand you were dealt. Make the most out of the situation and turn the bad circumstances around in your favor. Not everyone is born with a silver spoon in their mouth, but everyone can eventually end up eating off of silver plates if they do well enough with the circumstances that life dealt to them in certain situations in their life.

For Doc Rivers, he was dealt with what was possibly one of the worst and least talented collections of players in league history. Despite the circumstance that he was dealt with, Rivers did not allow himself to succumb to the situation. Instead, he turned it around in his favor by playing with whatever cards he had in his hand. He did the most with what was dealt to him.

Doc Rivers knew that his team sorely lacked in talent. Instead of just letting his team lose games due to the adverse circumstance of having zero All-Star talent, he designed a team that played collectively instead of individually. The Orlando Magic played an up-tempo style that relied on their running ability to score points. Any NBA player can run and score points in a hurry.

The defensive end was where Rivers focused that season. He made his team scrap and fight for every possession. The Orlando Magic pressured ball handlers for extra possessions and easy scoring opportunities. He made his team rely on their heart and their hustle for every win they earned that season.

A good leader such as Doc Rivers does not stress over things that are well beyond his control. The roster makeup was not his call, and he had no say in it. And because of that, he did not stress on what he lacked. He focused on what he could control and the hand he was given. What Doc Rivers could control was how his players would come out and play and react to any situation put before them. A good leader focuses on what he could control and what his players or people can do rather than what he could not control and what his players or people could not do.

3. Play as a Team

Four players were undrafted in the starting lineup that Doc Rivers fielded during the 1999-2000 season. In the starting lineup, the only recognizable players were Darrell Armstrong and Ben Wallace. Armstrong was a borderline starter at best. For most of his career, he was a serviceable backup point guard. On the other hand, Wallace would later win many Defensive Player of the Year awards and become an All-Star. But at that point of his career, he was still yet to blossom and break out. He was also an undrafted player in the 1996 NBA Draft.

The rest of Doc Rivers' roster was made up of unknowns and journeymen. He had as much as 19 players that season thanks to multiple transactions that the Orlando Magic front office made to clear up cap space. With different players coming in and out of the roster almost every week, Doc Rivers never forgot to let his team play united and as a whole.

Doc Rivers forced his players to care. They cared enough to learn their other teammates' skills and tendencies. They cared enough to focus on winning as a unit. They cared about playing together. And best of all, they cared about their fellow teammates. It was that sense of care that Doc Rivers thought made his job easy that season.

Of course, every leader would want to have an incredibly talented person on his team. However, no man can ever get a team job done all by himself. One person can make a huge difference on a team. But as an individual, that man himself can never be the team. Because of that, even the best individual performers should play and work as a team. And when you have a group of people that underperform on their own, the team can overachieve by making all of them care enough to work together united.

4. **Enjoy Yourself**

What is the purpose of doing something if at the end of the day, you do not enjoy it and stay unhappy? For Doc Rivers, he always kept his head high and enjoyed the ride of what was thought to be a disaster of a season for the Orlando Magic. All the negativity and pessimism went through his ears as he focused on enjoying the job and the positive side of coaching that team.

The Orlando Magic went along with him. The Magic played like they enjoyed making people eat their words. Every win they piled up that season made doubters and naysayers look like fools. The team enjoyed winning and keeping their heads up high for what was thought to be an impossible goal to achieve. The destination is only as important as the journey itself. And for the Orlando Magic, they enjoyed the journey they had that season despite falling short of their goal.

Good leaders know that leadership is not a burden to bear but a privilege to enjoy. Doc Rivers enjoyed such a privilege of coaching a team of underdogs to what was almost a playoff season for them. Instead of going along with the doomsday predictions that external voices were saying about the team, he kept his positive approach and enjoyed whatever wins and lessons he got that season. A leader should love the task of leading itself. Not everyone gets to be a leader. So if there is a chance to become one, grab it and enjoy it.

The Ubuntu Philosophy

After that Heart and Hustle season with the Orlando Magic, Doc Rivers would acquire a superstar in the form of Tracy McGrady. For much of his remaining years in Orlando, Doc Rivers' Magic teams relied mainly on the superstar prowess of T-Mac, though they were still some semblances of the team efforts and unity that made the 1999-2000 Orlando Magic a special team.

The same was also true when Doc Rivers moved to Boston to coach the Celtics. Paul Pierce was a one-man show that struggled to get his team to the playoffs. In his first three years with the Celtics, Rivers only made the postseason once due to a variety of factors such as injuries and roster instability. It was only during the 2007-08 season that Doc Rivers emerged as an elite coach with a precise philosophy and belief in coaching.

Back in 2002, Doc Rivers met a certain Kita 'Thierry' Matungulu, a philanthropist that helped established African basketball organizations that focus on teaching young children the importance of sports. They would meet at a fundraiser in New York when they were sitting together in one table. It was then and there when Rivers first heard about "Ubuntu."

Doc Rivers would read and learn more about Ubuntu by reading works by Bishop Desmond Tutu and the famous historical figure Nelson Mandela. According to

Mandela, Ubuntu had no exact meaning. It can be roughly translated to "I am because we are." However, the message of Ubuntu is universal. It teaches people of how much important it is to have a sense of community and unity. It embodies respect for one another and how sharing gifts and blessings make the community better off. For those who embody Ubuntu, it is never spoken, but rather only lived.[v]

According to Mandela, the spirit of Ubuntu was something they never spoke of but was merely done and lived. People walk through villages and villagers would give food and water without even being asked to do so or asking anything in return.[v] It was an inherent belief and mantra amongst the South African people. They believed in the sense of community that encompasses any individualistic ideal.

The first time that Doc Rivers mentioned the word was in one of the Boston Celtics' early practices. Rivers would mention the word again and again to the team without even having so much as to explain what Ubuntu meant. Players asked, but he never answered. He had his players, even the best of them, wait an entire day before he told them the meaning.[vi]

Instead of choosing his veterans and his Big Three, Doc Rivers decided to explain the word to his rookies knowing that such youngsters would never become skeptical or would not mind learning or hearing about a new philosophy. The rookies enthusiastically taught what they knew about Ubuntu to the veterans. The entire team would take it in with open minds.[vi]

After learning more about Ubuntu by reading the works of Tutu and Mandela, Doc Rivers would call Matungulu to ask him if it could be applied to basketball. Matungulu was not hesitant in asking the coach if he could go over to talk to the Celtics himself. After all, he was an inspirational speaker that preached the concept of Ubuntu for a living.[v]

Since 2007, Matungulu spends time with all of Doc Rivers' teams to talk about Ubuntu and expounds more on how the team can be more focused on such an ideal and philosophy. It became the Boston Celtics' battle cry and mantra from 2007 up until the time that Doc Rivers left the team in 2013. Rivers credits the philosophy for his lone championship ring in 2008.

For Doc Rivers, the philosophy of Ubuntu applies to basketball in the sense that the team should throw away any individualistic approaches. It was about sharing the team experience with everyone on the team. The veterans and Big Three shared the joy of victory with the young ones and rookies. In line with that, they also shared each other's pains and sacrifices. Along the way, they began sharing everything, not only on the hard floor, but also outside the court. The Boston Celtics took the sense of community with them to the NBA Finals when they won their first title since 1986.

The philosophy of Ubuntu lived in how the Boston Celtics played. On the offensive end, nobody dominated the possessions. The Big Three all played equally important roles. The veterans shared their knowledge and experiences with the younger players. The role players stepped up when they were needed. And on the defensive end, nobody could contend with how the Celtics ferociously frustrated their opponents by helping each other out and communicating properly on the floor.

Even as the Boston Celtics' core aged, Ubuntu lived on properly. In 2013, they were able to force seven games out of the younger and more talented Miami Heat Big Three by playing their brand of united basketball. Everyone put the team first before any other individualistic goals or endeavors. Their defense was sharp and on point as everyone on the team put the thought of others before them when defending their matchups.

While Ubuntu was short-lived for only six seasons in Boston, it continued to live on with the Los Angeles Clippers when Doc Rivers moved on to coach them. Doc Rivers hardly mentions the word to the Clippers. He was always careful enough to coach them differently because he believed that the Clippers' roster had different players that had different strengths and personalities. However, like the South African people, Ubuntu went on to live unspoken in Los Angeles.[v]

Doc Rivers always mentions the team concept with the Clippers. He even brought along Matungulu in one of their training camps to talk about the importance of sharing and playing as a community. Pretty soon, everyone in the locker room cared more about the other person than they did about themselves. There is no one dominant player on the Clippers' roster. Nobody cares about who dominated one game or another. What everyone was about more was the importance of how well they played as a team. As Blake Griffin said, nobody eats unless everyone gets to eat. In such a simple gesture, everyone got to feel the sense of community and sharing that is often preached by the philosophy of Ubuntu.

The Voice of Motivation

Doc Rivers has often been described as the ultimate player's coach and a master motivator. He has often maximized the abilities of his players and gets the best out of them by motivating them to do better on the court and to move past their limitations and fulfill their potential. Rivers always had that kind of a leadership trait since he first started as a head coach.

A lot, if not all of Doc Rivers' players, have excelled under his direction and coaching. The best example of players that have exceeded expectations through Rivers' motivational skills were those that played under him in the Orlando Magic during the 1999-2000 season. None of Doc Rivers' players that season were thought of as achievers or potentially talented. His best player was Darrell Armstrong, who was a borderline starter at best. Despite that, Rivers motivated a group of role players into a .500 season simply by getting the best out of them through his words and inspirational methods.

When the Orlando Magic signed Tracy McGrady in 2000, Doc Rivers finally had a star to work with. While everyone already knew how much potential T-Mac had in himself, it was only when he played under Rivers when he blossomed into one of the best stars in the league. But Doc Rivers would initially call the signing of McGrady as "blind faith" on the part of the Orlando Magic. After all, T-Mac was yet to grow into the potential everyone knew he had.

However, when Doc Rivers allowed Tracy McGrady to become a star after Grant Hill was unable to play for the Magic in his first season, the then-young star blossomed into one of premier wing men in the NBA and would lead the Orlando Magic to a playoff spot. However, Rivers would credit all of the Magic's performances to how McGrady led them at the age of 21 years old. But T-Mac would not have been such a great player for Orlando had Rivers not put his faith in him. T-Mac would have his best individual seasons in the years he played for the Magic under Doc Rivers.[vii]

When Doc Rivers moved to coach the Boston Celtics, Paul Pierce was his lone star, just like how T-Mac was his only prominent player in Orlando. At the peak of his career, Pierce was motivated by Rivers to play the best brand of basketball he has ever played in his time in the NBA. Just like T-Mac, all of Pierce's best statistical seasons was when he was the lone star in Boston under Rivers.

Despite playing his best individual seasons under Rivers, Paul Pierce initially could not see eye to eye with Doc, especially during his first season as the Boston Celtics' head coach. The inspirational head coach did not adjust to how Pierce wanted to play. Instead, he spoke to the star in front of the entire team and asked him to change because he (Rivers) was not going to modify the way he coached the team and the way he thought Pierce was supposed to play.[viii]

The two legendary Boston figures would eventually see eye to eye with Paul Pierce making most of the adjustments. It was when the Boston Celtics defeated the Detroit Pistons in the 2008 playoffs when Paul Pierce came up to Doc Rivers and told his coach that he was thankful he never changed. It was Rivers' insistence on not changing and motivate Paul Pierce to change for the better that eventually led to the star's great performance in winning the 2008 Finals MVP and the 2008 NBA championship.

In 2010, Doc Rivers was coaching an aging Celtics lineup that he still thought had enough to make the NBA Finals. He knew that the LA Lakers would be the ones getting out of the West to make the NBA Finals. The team would visit Los Angeles for a game during February of that year. They would win that bout, but

Doc Rivers was not content with a mere regular season win. Instead, he found a way to motivate his players to one day return to Staples Center to play the Lakers in the Finals.

After that win, Doc Rivers asked all of the players on the roster to give him $100. At first, he could not tell them what he was up to. When he asked $100 from Kevin Garnett, the Big Ticket was hesitant. For Rivers, it was like pulling a tooth out of him. He had to tell Garnett was he was up to. Rivers planned on taking the money out of all of his players to hide it somewhere in the visiting team's locker room for them to one day get the money back when they made the NBA Finals.[viii]

Through motivation and extra hard work, Rivers coached the Celtics back to the championship series that year against no less than the Lakers, who he always believed would make it to the Finals. And when they got to the locker room for Game 1, the money he had hidden was still there. The prophecy that Doc Rivers made in February came true just by adding a bit of motivation to his players.[viii]

Chapter 4: How Doc Rivers Maximizes Player Talent

Player Relationship

One of the principal foci of Doc Rivers as a head coach is to take care of his relationship with his players. He has always viewed relationship more than almost every other factor that an NBA coach should look at. He takes care of his relationship with his players, considering it as the main reason for the team's future success. That is why he treats his players with respect, and outside of the court, he always defends them when they are wrongly criticized.[ix]

Often described as the ultimate player's coach, Doc Rivers knows how important it is for coaches and players to have a good relationship. After all, he spent several years as a valued point guard under famed head coaches such as Mike Fratello, Larry Brown, Pat Riley, and Gregg Popovich. He was a player in the league, and he knows how his personnel would feel about certain coaching decisions and actions. As they say, it takes one to know one. Doc Rivers knows his players because he was once one, too.

One approach that Doc Rivers uses to take care of his relationships with players is that they allow them to be who they are. As his backup guard in Boston Keyon Dooling once said, Rivers never tried to change his players' attitude. He did not impose so many rules as to restrict and restrain his players' actions. Dooling once also recalled that Rivers never limited his players' movements during trips. He always gave them as much leeway as needed as long as they did their job well.[x]

Another approach he uses is to earn his players' trust. Trust and relationships go a long way. The more a person trusts another, the better the relationship. This much Doc Rivers knows. Rivers earns the trust he rightfully deserves by putting his players in positions where they could succeed as individuals and as a team. Seeing as how some of his players have grown to become stars and good contributors (Rondo, Perkins, and Tony Allen come to mind), the locker room tends to believe in his system and what he can bring to the table.

For his part, Kevin Garnett never liked playing the center position ever since he came into the league. Though he always had the size and skill to play center, he particularly hated it when coaches asked him to move up to that spot. However, Garnett would learn to trust Doc Rivers after playing less than a season for him back in 2007. He trusted Rivers enough to play the center position whenever his coach asked him to do it.

Garnett said that he would do anything for Doc Rivers knowing that whatever he was asked to do would not be for the purpose of harming him or making him look bad. He said that Rivers always cares about his players' health, body, and personal time. That was what made him a player's coach. That was how Garnett learned to trust him. For Garnett, he never thought that Rivers would say to him or to tell him to do anything that would be wrong for him. That was how much he trusted Doc Rivers.[x]

Doc Rivers also earns his players' trust by learning how to trust them himself. Kevin Garnett once called the Boston Celtics coaching staff "Cuba" because he believed it was a dictatorship ruled by Doc Rivers. He meant to say that Rivers was the alpha and the omega whenever it came to making coaching decisions. But behind all that, Rivers allowed the players to own the locker room. The on-court duties were things that Rivers limited to himself, but he trusted his players and allowed them to do what they wanted to do in the other aspects of the team. As Keyon Dooling said, Rivers enabled them to police themselves in the locker room like proper men would do.[x]

Doc Rivers also takes care of his relationship with players by making sure he rarely indicted them in criticisms and issues that would adversely affect locker room chemistry. However, when needed to, he would call his players out or tell them to make sacrifices, especially when he knows it is for the betterment of the team. Rivers consistently calls out the name of players that are out of shape. And when he asked Garnett to play the center spot and Allen to come off the bench, it did not sit well with them, but they did it anyway because that was what the coach perceived as what would make the team better.[x]

Doc Rivers values player relationship so much that, when he coached the Clippers, he consistently brought in players that he had a chance to coach before when he was with the Celtics. He has since signed Paul Pierce, Nate Robinson, Glen Davis, and Jeff Green, among other former Celtics players. He has even brought in Kevin Garnett as a team consultant. He has made such decisions as coach and GM of the Clippers, particularly because of the level of trust and relationship he has formed with his former players. He would even sign his son Austin Rivers because he has had a good relationship with the young guard since the day he was born back in 1992.[xi]

The Keys to Talent Maximization

Doc Rivers employed J.P. Clark, a coach that specializes in player development, in both his time as the head coach of the Celtics and when he moved on to the LA Clippers. Rivers leaves a lot of the development tasks to Clark, who believes that no NBA player has ever wanted to become mediocre or has ever settled for less than what they could. He also believes that the raw talent that size, athleticism, and strength provide are only complementary to how a player works hard to unleash his full potential. And in maximizing a player's potential, J.P. Clark presented five keys:[xii]

1. The Best Athletes Have a Well-Defined "Why"

The best players and athletes all have a purpose as to why they play the game. They have mission statements and a vision as to how their careers will ultimately play out when all things have been said and done. Clark believes that the athlete and player must first establish and know the "why" and the reason he plays the game.

An athlete with a clear sense of purpose and reason will always be willing to fail in the minor things to achieve greater heights. When the player understands this, he will be prepared to go through every hardship just to get to his ultimate cause and reason for playing the game. It is this same purpose that provides an athlete with a sense of direction in his life. This is what gives him that fiery energy and love for the game.

Having a clear reason and purpose is something not exclusive for players. Every leader should know how to make his people move and act with a sense of direction and purpose because it is those very things that fuel his passion for succeeding and making the most out of his abilities.

2. The Best Athletes Have a Plan of Action

While knowing the "whys" is the initial step to maximizing talent, there must also be a clear plan of action on how to achieve that reason. There must be a "how." There must be an established plan that can help the player get from his initial position at point A to point B, his final goal and destination as an athlete.

One such way that Doc Rivers was able to maximize his roster's talent was to develop younger players while the veterans did the heavy lifting. Kendrick Perkins quietly and steadily improved as a premier defensive big man under the tutelage of Kevin Garnett precisely because of how Rivers wanted his veteran helping the young center achieve his goal as a force inside the paint. Meanwhile, Tony Allen became an elite defender while learning under guys like Ray Allen and James Posey. It was this kind of a veteran-youngster relationship that helped Rivers' players maximize their talents and skills while still contending for titles.

For coaches that focus on developing talent, it is always crucial to have a clear cut plan on how to get your personnel to achieve their reasons for playing. A leader should not only focus on the team's overall goal, but should also be able to help his team achieve their purposes along the way. That was how Rajon Rondo became an elite point guard in the league and how DeAndre Jordan and Kendrick Perkins improved as defenders.

3. The Best Athletes Outwork the Competition

   Hard work beats talent when talent does not work hard. But when a talented athlete works just as hard as those with less talent, he becomes one of the all-time greats. Talent alone cannot get a player from point A to point B. He must also learn how to outwork his competition, especially when his competition has more talent than he does.

The perfect example of a maniacal hard working talent is Kevin Garnett. Garnett was always one of the most talented players in the league ever since he got drafted in 1995. But Kevin Garnett did not let his talent get him to a lone championship ring. He worked harder than any other power forward in the league in recent memory. He treats shootarounds seriously and just as intensely as he does when he is in an actual game.

Doc Rivers would once comment on how intense KG is in every facet of the game. On television, everybody can see how fiery Garnett can be on both ends of the floor. But Rivers would say that he is just as intense during practices as he is in games. His intensity and maniacal efforts never take breaks or days off. That kind of intensity and dedication to work hard has spread to the rest of the Celtics.

4. The Best Athletes Believe in Themselves

Those that want to maximize their potential would always believe that they could reach their goals and that they are talented and skillful enough to do so. No athlete has ever been great by refusing to believe in how truly good he is. There should never be negativity and doubt in a player that tries to seek his full capacity as an athlete.

One such player that Doc Rivers has had a chance to coach, Paul Pierce, always believed in how good he truly is. Pierce once proclaimed he was the greatest shooter on the planet. He would also consistently claim that nobody in the league could guard him. While his allegations may be argued with, it does not take away the fact that

Pierce's strong belief in himself took him to heights he would have never gotten to had he not had such self-confidence.

A great leader knows how to maximize talent by making his players believe they can do it. No leader or coach out there would tell their people to have zero confidence in themselves. Instead, a leader would always want to instill the value of self-confidence in his people so that they could achieve their maximum potential.

5. The Best Understand They Cannot Do It Alone—Become Lifelong Learners

"If you want to go fast, go alone. If you want to go far, go together." Those words are some of the best that Doc Rivers has ever uttered as a head coach. This goes back to his belief in the concept of Ubuntu, which stresses the importance of focusing on the community mindset and on sharing rather than individual success and achievements. Rivers always believes that no one player can do everything alone. To get far in the league, a player must understand that he cannot do it alone and that he needs others to achieve his maximum potential.

In a team setup, a leader should always stress teamwork over individual success. Many players have reached their full potential, not by relying mainly on themself, but also by relying on what their teammates and coaches can do. Michael Jordan and LeBron James could not win titles on their own despite the fact that they were stellar players individually. Instead, they needed other players to help them get to their best performing states. And in Boston as well as LA, Doc Rivers' three best players in both teams all complement each other in such ways that they become better individual players by relying on how good the others are. After all, basketball is a team sport. No player or person can become great without having to rely on others at some point in time.

The Challenge

What was one of the most glaring parts of Doc Rivers' way of getting his players to perform at the highest level is by always challenging them to excel in certain situations in front of them. The moment he started coaching in 1999, Rivers was consistently challenging players to make the most out of their talents and the expectations put on their shoulders.

It started during the 1999-2000 season when Doc Rivers was but a rookie head coach trying to lead what was then considered the worst team ever assembled on paper. Doc Rivers challenged a group of role players and rejects to ignore the early predictions and expectations. Instead, he challenged them to try and win every game they played through heart and hustle. Pretty soon, everyone started believing they could beat the best teams to the point that they would get frustrated after losses.[i]

When Tracy McGrady joined the Orlando Magic in 2000, Doc Rivers challenged him to become a superstar his potential has always dictated him to be. Rivers challenged T-Mac to become a do-it-all star like Scottie Pippen was. Instead, McGrady was even better. Not only did he pass and rebound, but he was also one of the best scorers of his time. Tracy McGrady did everything on the floor with such precision and talent that he was gunning for the title of the league's best player at one point in his career.

However, Doc Rivers still believes to this day that Tracy McGrady was put in a situation that harmed his long-term career. He was still at his formative years as a star during his time with the Magic. Rivers wanted him to be the Pippen to Grant Hill's Jordan. However, Hill never got to play for more than half of a season in the three years he spent in Orlando. Because of that, T-

Mac had to become 1986-87 Michael Jordan in the several years he spent with the Magic. The pain of being a selfish player when you are unselfish was too much of a burden for McGrady to bear in those seasons.[xiii]

When Doc Rivers went to Boston in 2004, he would consistently butt heads with superstar Paul Pierce throughout the entire season because of how they could not see eye-to-eye. Rivers thought Pierce should play another way while the star forward believed he should play the same way he has been playing since he came to the league. Doc Rivers would, later on, challenge Paul Pierce in front of the entire team to change the way he played because he (Rivers) would not change his way of coaching Pierce. Pierce would realize the value of the challenge when he began playing with Garnett and Allen.

And in his first season as the head coach of the Los Angeles Clippers, Doc Rivers issued a challenge to center DeAndre Jordan. Before Rivers' arrival, Jordan was simply a center that relied on his athletic ability more than his hunger to compete and play the position the best way he could. Rivers challenged him to become a defensive beast, if not the best defensive center in the league.

DeAndre Jordan responded by nearly doubling his rebounding averages and by averaging a double-double in points and rebounds that season. He became the Clippers' intimidating force in the middle because of how well he defended the paint, grabbed rebounds, and finished plays when the ball found him under the basket or over the rim.[xiv] DeAndre Jordan has since then become an All-NBA First Team member and an All-Star.

Just recently, the Los Angeles Clippers have been losing games because of how they lose their composure during tight situations. The Clippers consistently rank as one of the top teams concerning technical fouls because of how they are easily flustered. Doc Rivers once realized this problem and challenged his team to hold their tongues and eliminate the ridiculous number of technical fouls they had been getting. Rivers told them that they would not get the results they desired if they did not change the way they act. And because of that, the Clippers have lessened their emotional outbursts on the court and have since then played more under control.[xv]

By consistently challenging his players to different results and diverse situations, Doc Rivers has been getting the most of their talent. Ever the motivator and the player's coach, Rivers knows what kinds of challenges could make players perform better than they ever did precisely because he has also been in similar situations. It is that kind of an experience and trait that has helped him make even the least talented players into productive ones in all the teams he has coached.

Chapter 5: Doc Rivers' System

Most other NBA head coaches rely on a clear-cut system for extended periods of time. Phil Jackson always runs the triangle offense in every kind of situation. Mike D'Antoni's run-and-gun style focuses on getting good shots up in a hurry. He has applied that style in all of his head coaching stops. Meanwhile, Steve Kerr relies on a free-wheeling offensive style that focuses on reading and reacting to the opposing team's defense.

But for Doc Rivers, his system relies more on how he adjusts his rotations and matchups rather than sticking to a precise system. His style has always depended on the personnel that he has. In his rookie season, he practically had nothing to deal with. Because of that, he focused more on his team's scrappiness and defensive intensity to carve out wins in what was thought to be a miraculous season for the Orlando Magic.

When Rivers acquired T-Mac in 2000, and when he started coaching the Boston Celtics in 2004, Rivers switched to a fast-paced offensive system that relied on offense and three-pointers. T-Mac was an unselfish player that attracted defenses and loved passing out to open shooter such as Mike Miller, Pat Garrity, and Gordan Giriček, among others. And with Paul Pierce, he had shooters like Antoine Walker, Wally Szczerbiak, and Ricky Davis sniping from the three-point line. But at that point in his coaching career, Doc Rivers was often the subject of criticism. Fans and analysts would call out for his ouster from Boston because his system and approach did not work for the Magic or the Celtics.

In 2007, Doc Rivers would change his approach when he acquired two other Hall of Famers to flank Paul Pierce. Together with other veteran acquisitions, he would build on the two pillars that made Gregg Popovich's teams consistent title contenders. Those pillars are defensive intensity and ball distribution.[xvi]

He believed that the personnel he had were experienced and unselfish enough to stand by those pillars. He was right.

On the defensive end of the floor, he had two great inside anchors in Kevin Garnett and Kendrick Perkins. KG himself was an excellent defensive communicator, who always made sure his teammates were rotating and aware of switches and matchups on the floor. Relying on such a strong defender like Garnett, Doc Rivers had his team play with the same kind of fiery passion on the defensive end. His players were scrapping for loose balls and pressuring ball handlers.

Defensive specialists Tom Thibodeau and Lawrence Frank helped Doc Rivers in implementing this kind of a scheme to the Celtics. That defensive style focuses on pressure and on encouraging one-on-one plays by taking away driving and passing lanes. Because of this, other scoring options are forced to become more creative by looking for screens and cutting more often than they did.

Rivers' defensive scheme also takes away options for the ball handler. By crowding the lane and overloading on the strong side to take away passing lanes, ball handlers are forced to reset the play or to take tough contested shots over his defender. This was how the Boston Celtics consistently made it tough for LeBron James to get past the Eastern Conference in his first run with the Cavs.[xvii]

Since 2007, the Boston Celtics consistently found themselves atop the list of the NBA's best defensive teams. They were always tops regarding defensive rating while also frustrating teams into scoring the lowest amount of points for several consecutive years. It was this kind of defensive style that made the Celtics consistent title contenders.

On the offensive end, Doc Rivers stressed the concept of Ubuntu. By believing in Ubuntu, the Celtics were unselfish on the offensive end of the floor despite having three great scorers in Garnett, Pierce, and Allen, all three of whom could easily average 20 points a night if they wanted to. Instead, the Boston Big Three were the role models of unselfishness for the Celtics. They were passing the ball fluidly on offense to make sure everyone had a chance to score the ball.

When Doc Rivers' Celtics teams changed over the years, he would adjust accordingly by changing matchups and shortening his rotations. At some point later in his time with Boston, he would even put Ray Allen on the bench to start perimeter defense specialist Avery Bradley. He would also put Kevin Garnett on the center position to match up well with NBA teams that have increasingly been leaning towards smaller and faster lineups.

When he moved to Los Angeles to coach the Clippers, Doc Rivers made sure he did not treat his new team the same way as he did with Boston precisely because he believed that the two teams had different personnel and skills. He would lean back to a faster offensive-oriented style of play that still leaned towards the two pillars of basketball coaching.

On the offensive end, having a Hall of Fame point guard Chris Paul in the prime of his career and athletic frontcourt players like Blake Griffin and DeAndre Jordan meant that Doc Rivers could play the Clippers faster. Relying on several staggered screens and baseline cuts, he took advantage of his personnel's ability to pass the ball to get easy and open shots for his players. For several years, the Clippers would consistently rank atop the NBA in offensive rating.

Doc Rivers also used the same kind of defensive style he employed in Boston when he went to LA. However, knowing he did not have the same kind of personnel, he tweaked it a little. Instead of letting his big men pack the paint as a deterrent for those willing to challenge them in the middle, Rivers would allow both

Griffin and Jordan to come out and show out to the ball handler. They knew that they could both get back to their original positions faster than both Garnett and Perkins could back in Boston. He would also encourage his big men to switch out on pick-and-rolls considering that they could also cover the perimeter. And instead of focusing on letting his players crash the boards, he would make them run back on defense knowing that his big men could rebound and get back on the defensive end faster than most others could.

In summary, Doc Rivers' system is an ever-evolving one because he believes that different sets of players and skills need different sets of plays and styles. Whenever he faced drastic roster changes or switched to other teams, Rivers always changed the way he approached his players because of how he thought his new personnel was different from the last one. It is this kind of an open mindset that has allowed Doc Rivers to stay as one of the elite coaches in the league.

Chapter 6: Key Takeaways

Ubuntu

One of Doc Rivers' primary gifts to the world of basketball was the introduction of the philosophy of Ubuntu. As already explained, Ubuntu is a term that roughly translates to "I am because we are." While the term has a rough translation, Nelson Mandela would say that it does not have a precise meaning because it encompasses the concept of community, sharing, unselfishness, and commitment to one another. Ubuntu is something to be lived and not to be believed.

When the Celtics acquired both Kevin Garnett and Ray Allen, Ubuntu became their battle cry towards dominance and in their quest for the 2008 NBA championship. Rivers thought that Ubuntu fit well with the personnel that they had. He wanted his players to believe in the common goal of winning a title for one another.

At that moment in the Celtics' life, there was a sense of community in the way the team played on both offense and defense. Offensively, nobody dominated the possessions and the shot attempts. Everybody shared the ball and passed it around to find the best available shot. On defense, the Boston Celtics moved like a well-oiled machine. Their defensive schemes reacted well to how the opposing team adjusted their offense. Everybody communicated well as the Celtics looked like a single defensive machine, wherein one cog moves the others are quick to react.

Despite not using it as his motto, Doc Rivers would also bring several concepts of Ubuntu when he went to the Los Angeles Clippers. The Clippers would move the ball well on offense on the common belief that everybody should be able to contribute and score. On the defensive end was where LA improved from their time with Vinny Del Negro. The Clippers read and reacted well to offenses while communicating better than they ever did before because of how Rivers preached the importance of acting as one unit and one community.

While teamwork and unity are all basic concepts in any sport, the difference in what Ubuntu has brought to the way Doc Rivers coached his teams is that it is a lifestyle that has to be lived. In South Africa, Ubuntu was already inherent in the minds of its people. They hardly talked about it, but would always act in accordance to what it stands for without having to be asked to do it. This kind of philosophy was what Doc Rivers wanted to bring to his teams. He never wanted to continuously preach teamwork and unity because believing in Ubuntu means you never have to be asked to be unselfish. You just have to do it inherently and wholeheartedly.

Motivating by Challenging

Doc Rivers was always described as the ultimate players' coach and one of the best motivators that the NBA has to offer. Rivers was just as good at emotionally preaching his players as he was in strategically mapping out plays. He would find out that the best way he could motivate his players was to consistently challenge them to get better and perform more than what they could do.

Back in his first season in Orlando, he challenged a group of outcasts and rejects by telling them to ignore external expectations and believe that they could beat any team in the NBA no matter what analysts or papers said about their talent level. They exceeded all expectations precisely because of how Rivers challenged them to silence naysayers and doubters by focusing on playing with hustle and heart every game.

Rivers has also brought out the best in some of his star players by challenging them to fulfill their true potential. Tracy McGrady broke out as a superstar when he was challenged to take his talents to the next level and lead the Orlando Magic as if it was his team. He challenged Paul Pierce to change the way he played so that the Celtics would become an even better team under his leadership. He would then challenge DeAndre Jordan to rise above expectations and hone his natural talents to become one of the best inside defenders in the entire league.

It is by throwing out challenges to his players and teams that Doc Rivers was able to track how much they react to the changes and developments that he wanted them to cover. By consistently challenging his personnel, Rivers can keep the competitive fuel burning inside his players as they are also trying to get to the level needed for them to win while making sure that they were also playing to the tune of what their coach wanted them to do.

Treasuring Relationships

The ultimate player's coach's key to relating better to his players than most other coaches do is that he makes sure he takes care of the trust and confidence given to him by his personnel. Doc Rivers has always treasured his relationships with the players that have played under him. He puts player relationship above all else because that is where the foundation of trust comes from. Players that do not trust the coach and system tend to be cancerous to the team and what it stands for.

By trusting the players and believing in their maturity as decision makers, Doc Rivers has also gained the confidence of his players. Almost everyone he has had the chance to coach have bought into the system and the teachings he has been planting in the minds of his players and team. It takes a certain level of trust in the coach to do what he wants you to do without hesitation under the belief that whatever he does is for the betterment of the entire team. Rivers has earned that level of trust from his players, and that is why his style was never openly questioned by his teams.

Throughout the years, Doc Rivers has developed key relationships with players that have helped him along the way. Paul Pierce has since become one of his favorite players and helped him when he signed with the Clippers despite his advanced age. Through the bond and trust he has formed with Rivers back in Boston, Kevin Garnett helps the Clippers as an adviser and as a consultant.

And on a much more different case, he once coached Ty Lue, who is now the head coach of the Cleveland Cavaliers. Before leaving Orlando, he once told Lue that he believed he had what it took to become a coach. After Lue retired, Rivers immediately took him in under his wing on the basis of the relationship they formed back in Orlando. Lue would learn from Doc the ability to call out a player and challenge him to do better. Back in 2016, Ty Lue would openly challenge LeBron James to tap into his old MVP self and try to bring the Cavaliers to the Promised Land on the strength of his strong shoulders. Ultimately, LeBron would win the Finals MVP of the 2016 championship series and has been openly telling the world how much he trusts Lue particularly because of how he is consistently challenged to do better.

It is how Doc Rivers keeps and treasures relationships with people he has had a chance to work with that has made the difference when it comes to players choosing to sign with his team and staff opting to work under him. A player would indeed be crazy not to want to play for a coach that not only consistently challenges you to get better but also believes in your inherent ability to become greater than you ever were as a player. It is in this sense that Doc Rivers has been known to be the consummate player's coach and one of the best coaches of his era.

Conclusion

Despite not having the number of rings that his other contemporaries have and despite not having as colorful a resume as other championship coaches have, Doc Rivers is still one of the top coaches in the NBA. This is because of the overall package he brings to the table, not only as a strategically sound tactician but also as a fundamental leader that takes player relationship and unity seriously.

Rivers has been wrongly criticized over the past years. He has been called overrated. He has been called lucky to have had a chance to coach three Hall of Famers. And he has also been called a has-been because of how his style has not seen great results with the Clippers. However, the fact that Rivers has been in the NBA for a very long time handling superstar and All-Star egos and having them mesh together to form contenders is what has made him one of the best coaches of this era.

While Pierce, Garnett, and Allen were all great individual players, it took more than talent to take them to the Promised Land after only one season. It took what Doc Rivers was preaching for them to accept their differences and learn to play harmoniously together as a strong defensive unit that relied on each other more than anything else. No other coach could have quickly bonded those three players faster than how Rivers did it.

And with the Clippers, nobody could argue how much depth and talent they have as a unit. Doc Rivers took that talent to greater heights by challenging them to get better and by focusing on his best players' strengths instead of their weaknesses. Rivers turned Paul back into the 20-10 playmaker he used to be back in New Orleans by trusting in what the point guard could do on the offensive end. He would make Blake Griffin into an all-around scoring, rebounding, and passing threat that none of his other past coaches were able to do. Then he would turn DeAndre Jordan into an elite center in the NBA simply by challenging him and by harnessing all that raw talent into something that worked well with the Clippers.

Arguably Doc Rivers' biggest opponent as a head coach were all the injuries his key players suffered. He would have had one of the greatest combination of wing players had Grant Hill been healthy in Orlando. He could have won back-to-back title rings had Garnett been healthy in 2009. Many argued he would have also owned the 2010 NBA Finals had Kendrick Perkins been available for Game 7. And with the Clippers, in-season injuries to both Chris Paul and Blake Griffin the past two years have caused him losses in both the regular season and the playoffs. Had his core been healthy the entire time in those two seasons, the Los Angeles Clippers would have given the other elite teams a run for their money. Who knows? He might have even won a title with the Clippers had the stars aligned in their favor.

With those said and done, nobody can take away the fact that Doc Rivers is and has been one of the best coaches in the NBA for nearly two decades now. From winning Coach of the Year to hoisting the Larry O'Brien trophy, Doc Rivers has seen it all and has been consistently turning seasons around and improving his players ever since he donned the head coach's mantle in 1999. As he is still comparatively young as an NBA coach, Doc Rivers still has a lot of years left. And with the way he coaches his teams to become consistent contenders, nobody can ever laugh at the thought that he would someday find a partner for that lone title ring he won when he was still in Boston.

Final Word/About the Author

I was born and raised in Norwalk, Connecticut. Growing up, I could often be found spending many nights watching basketball, soccer, and football matches with my father in the family living room. I love sports and everything that sports can embody. I believe that sports are one of most genuine forms of competition, heart, and determination. I write my works to learn more about influential athletes and coaches in the hopes that from my writing, you the reader can walk away inspired to put in an equal if not greater amount of hard work and perseverance to pursue your goals. If you enjoyed *Doc Rivers*, please leave a review! Also, you can read more of my works on *Roger Federer*, *Novak Djokovic*, *Andrew Luck*, *Rob Gronkowski*, *Brett Favre*, *Calvin Johnson*, *Drew Brees*, *J.J. Watt*, *Colin Kaepernick*, *Aaron Rodgers*, *Peyton Manning*, *Tom Brady*, *Russell Wilson*, *Michael Jordan*, *LeBron James*, *Kyrie Irving*, *Klay Thompson*, *Stephen Curry*, *Kevin Durant*, *Russell Westbrook*,

Anthony Davis, Chris Paul, Blake Griffin, Kobe Bryant, Joakim Noah, Scottie Pippen, Carmelo Anthony, Kevin Love, Grant Hill, Tracy McGrady, Vince Carter, Patrick Ewing, Karl Malone, Tony Parker, Allen Iverson, Hakeem Olajuwon, Reggie Miller, Michael Carter-Williams, John Wall, James Harden, Tim Duncan, Steve Nash, Draymond Green, Kawhi Leonard, Dwyane Wade, Ray Allen, Pau Gasol, Dirk Nowitzki, Jimmy Butler, Paul Pierce, Manu Ginobili, Pete Maravich, Larry Bird, Kyle Lowry, Jason Kidd, David Robinson, LaMarcus Aldridge, Derrick Rose, Paul George, Kevin Garnett, Chris Paul, Marc Gasol, Yao Ming, Al Horford, Amar'e Stoudemire, DeMar DeRozan, Isaiah Thomas, Kemba Walker and Chris Bosh in the Kindle Store. If you love basketball, check out my website at claytongeoffreys.com to join my exclusive list where I let you know about my latest books and give you lots of goodies.

Like what you read? Please leave a review!

I write because I love sharing the stories of influential coaches like Doc Rivers with fantastic readers like you. My readers inspire me to write more so please do not hesitate to let me know what you thought by leaving a review! If you love books on life, basketball, or productivity, check out my website at claytongeoffreys.com to join my exclusive list where I let you know about my latest books. Aside from being the first to hear about my latest releases, you can also download a free copy of *33 Life Lessons: Success Principles, Career Advice & Habits of Successful People*. See you there!

Clayton

References

[i] Rossman-Reich. "Remembering Heart and Hustle". *Fan Sided*. 17 June 2014. Web

[ii] "Rivers is 16th Head Coach of Celtics". *ESPN*. 30 April 2004. Web

[iii] Barshad, Amos. "RIP, Ubuntu (2007-2013)". *Grant Land*. 24 June 2013. Web

[iv] Morris, Dr. Greg. "Leadership Lessons From the NBA". *Leadership Dynamics*. 7 August 2009. Web

[v] Markazi, Arash. "Ubuntu Philosophy Lives On With Clippers". *ESPN*. 6 December 2013. Web

[vi] Alden, Gerald. "I Am Because We Aare—Flashback on UBUNTU". *Celtics Life*. 19 July 2010. Web

[vii] Golliver, Ben. "Remembering Tracy McGrady's Career". *Sports Illustrated*. 27 August 2013. Web

[viii] Winter, Jack. "All The Amazing Stories Doc Rivers Told In His Recent 'Sports Illustrated' Feature". *Uproxx*. 9 November 2015. Web

[ix] Norof, Ethan. "Doc Rivers and the Most Underappreciated Coaches in the NBA". *Bleacher Report*. 23 May 2012. Web

[x] Flannery, Paul. "The Genius of Doc Rivers, a True Player's Coach". *WEEI*. 13 April 2012. Web

[xi] Sherman, Roger. "A History of Doc Rivers Acquiring Players He Saw Playing Well One Time". *SB Nation*. 19 February 2016. Web

[xii] Clark, J.P. "The 5 Keys to Fully Maximize Your Talent". *Better Basketball*. 6 July 2013. Web

[xiii] Simmons, Bill. "The Unfortunate Tale of T-Mac". *Grant Land*. 30 August 2013. Web

[xiv] Friedman, Oren. "Don't Look Now, But DeAndre Jordan is Rising to Doc Rivers' Challenge". *Bleacher Report*. 20 November 2013. Web

[xv] Woike, Dan. "Clippers' Doc Rivers Challenges Himself, His Players to Eliminate Technical Fouls". *Orange County Register*. 5 January 2017. Web

[xvi] Riccobondo, Anthony. "Why Doc Rivers Is A Better Coach Than Most People Think". *International Business Tmes*. 8 August 2012. Web

[xvii] Murphy, Dylan. "How Doc Rivers' Scheme Will Drastically

Improve the Clippers Defense". *Bleacher Report*. 3 August 2013. Web

Made in the USA
Coppell, TX
14 May 2023

16822915R10075